my best friend charlie

By Dana Seguin

Illustrated by Delaney O'Dell

Leaning Rock Press
Gales Ferry, CT

Leaning Rock Press
Gales Ferry, CT 06335
leaningrockpress@gmail.com
www.leaningrockpress.com

https://www.dsstudiocreative.com/

978-1-960596-80-2 (softcover)
978-1-960596-81-9 (Hardcover)

Library of Congress Control Number: 2025927373

Publisher's Cataloging-in-Publication Data
(Prepared by Cassidy Cataloguing's PCIP Service)

Names: Seguin, Dana, author. | O'Dell, Delaney, illustrator.
Title: My best friend Charlie / by Dana Seguin ; illustrated by Delaney O'Dell.
Description: Gales Ferry, CT : Leaning Rock Press, [2025] | Interest age level: 003-010. | Summary: My Best Friend Charlie by Dana Seguin is a touching, true story about a rescue dog who finds his forever home--and helps heal his new owner's heart in return ... From Charlie's timid beginnings to his adventures in New York and beyond, this story shows how love can help us all grow brave.--Publisher.
Identifiers: ISBN: 9781960596819 (hardcover) | 9781960596802 (softcover)
Subjects: LCSH: Dogs--Juvenile literature. | Dog adoption--Juvenile literature. | Human-animal relationships--Juvenile literature. | Friendship. | Courage--Juvenile literature. | CYAC: Dogs. | Dog adoption. Human-animal relationships. | Friendship. | Courage. | BISAC: JUVENILE NONFICTION / Animals / Dogs. | JUVENILE NONFICTION / Social Themes / Emotions & Feelings. | JUVENILE NONFICTION / Social Topics / Friendship.
Classification: LCC: PZ7.1.S338716 My 2025 | DDC: [E]--dc23

Printed in the United States of America

Dedicated to my best friend Charlie

Once upon a time Charlie was
being raised in a shelter.
He had never known a real home.

What Charlie didn't know was... someone else was feeling lonely too.

They didn't know it yet but they
were about to find each other.

At first Charlie was
scared, everything felt
strange and new.

But then... Charlie gave a little kiss.
And that's when I knew we'd be best
friends forever

"Let's go home Charlie."

9

Home was full of surprises. At first Charlie was even scared of the stairs.

But day by day,

we found our rhythm.

We walked together.

We cuddled.

We rode in the car,

side by side.

Then came a big adventure- a work trip to New York! Charlie came too.

12

At the photo shoot, all the models loved him.
They rubbed his belly, and he got more hugs than anyone!

13

14

Then something amazing happened...
Charlie was in the Christmas campaign!
His face was everywhere- on mailers, in stores, even in Times Square!

16

Little did we know...

Charlie had become a star!

But no matter where we went-
from New York to Atlanta-
Charlie was always by my side.

Then we moved again-
to a house in Ohio.
And there, Charlie got the biggest
surprise yet...

A new dad, and a sister named Reese!

Charlie never
expected it,
but he found more
than just a home.

23

He found a family!

Author's note

This is a true story of Charlie, a rescue dog who changed my life.

He was scared at first, but love
helped him grow brave.

I didn't just rescue Charlie-
he rescued me right back.

About the Author

Dana Seguin, a creative powerhouse in the world of fashion marketing, is celebrated for her bold ideas, fearless storytelling, and her commitment to building purpose-driven brands that inspire confidence and inclusivity. Over the course of her 25-year career, she has become known as a visionary leader in brand development, advertising, PR, and social media, with a keen ability to blend artistry and strategy in everything she touches.

Dana's work has helped shape the modern conversation around beauty and body positivity. Her creative influence can be seen in some of fashion's most beloved brands — including American Eagle, Aerie, and SPANX — where her campaigns have championed authenticity and redefined the way people see themselves and each other. Currently, as Chief Marketing Officer at Altar'd State, Dana leads with heart, imagination, and a belief that creativity can drive meaningful change.

Her debut book, My Best Friend Charlie, is a deeply personal project inspired by the kind of friendship that leaves a forever mark — a story that celebrates love, and the magic of connection. Beyond her professional achievements, Dana is known for her infectious energy, her love of storytelling in all forms, and her dedication to mentoring young creatives in the industry.

When she's not dreaming up her next big idea, Dana can usually be found with her pups, family, and with her signature red lip — always.

About the Illustrator

Hi I'm **Delaney O'Dell**! I live in Knoxville, TN with my two kitties, who keep me company while I work on all things creative. I moved here about three years ago from Orlando, FL to follow my passion for graphic design. I studied at Flagler College, which gave me a deep love for the beach—but since moving, I've grown just as fond of the mountains.

"My Best Friend Charlie" is the very first book I've illustrated, and I loved every step of bringing it to life. These days, I spend most of my time creating beautiful things for Altar'd State, while also diving into little side projects that keep my creativity flowing.

www.ingramcontent.com/pod-product-compliance
Lightning Source LLC
Chambersburg PA
CBHW041135120626
46547CB00019B/2996